D1435997

C334338815

BRIGHT
IDEA
BOOKS

HOW DO
Penguins
STAY
WARM?

Nancy Furstinger

raintree

a Capstone company — publishers for children

Raintree is an imprint of Capstone Global Library Limited, a company incorporated in England and Wales having its registered office at 264 Banbury Road, Oxford, OX2 7DY – Registered company number: 6695582

www.raintree.co.uk
myorders@raintree.co.uk

Edited by Maddie Spalding
Designed by Becky Daum
Production by Melissa Martin
Printed and bound in India

ISBN 978 1 4747 7515 1
22 21 20 19 18
10 9 8 7 6 5 4 3 2 1

British Library Cataloguing in Publication Data
A full catalogue record for this book is available from the British Library.

Acknowledgements
iStockphoto: JeremyRichards, 10–11, SteveAllenPhoto, 26–27, vladsilver, 12–13, 28; Science Source: Frans Lanting/MINT Images, 5; Shutterstock Images: Brandon B, 25, Enrique Aguirre, 16–17, Evannovostro, cover (background), Fredy Thuerig, 15, 31, Helene Sauvageot, 21, Kotomiti Okuma, cover (right foreground), Ondrej Prosicky, 22–23, Robert Bruce Lilley, 9, Roger Clark ARPS, cover (left foreground), Sergey 402, 6–7, Volodymyr Goinyk, 18–19
Design Elements: iStockphoto, Red Line Editorial, and Shutterstock Images

We would like to thank Heather J. Lynch, PhD, from the Department of Ecology & Evolution at Stony Brook University for her invaluable help in the preparation of this book.

CONTENTS

CHAPTER 1

MAKING a Wave

It's another chilly day in Antarctica. The temperature is −18°C (0°F). Thousands of emperor penguins huddle together. Penguin **chicks** are tucked under their parents' **pouches**. This keeps them warm.

Huddling keeps emperor penguins warm during snowstorms and cold weather.

New penguins join the huddle. They take small steps every 30 to 60 seconds. But they always stay together. They share their body heat. This keeps them warm.

Penguins take turns moving into the middle of the huddle. That is the warmest spot. The moving penguins look like a wave.

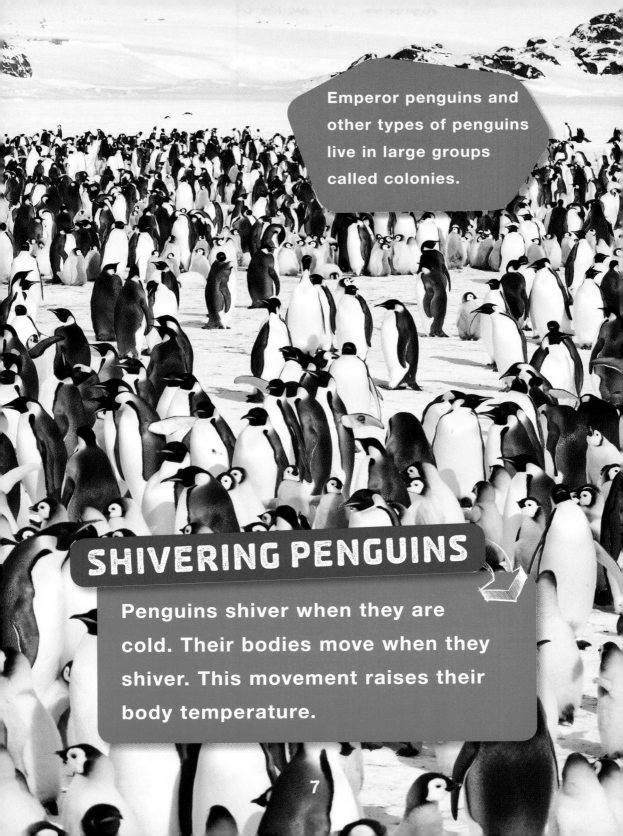

Emperor penguins and other types of penguins live in large groups called colonies.

SHIVERING PENGUINS

Penguins shiver when they are cold. Their bodies move when they shiver. This movement raises their body temperature.

CHAPTER 2

ANTARCTIC
Penguins

Many penguins live in cold places. About 12 million penguins live in Antarctica. The Antarctic ice is chilly. Winds whip across the land. Storms bring snow.

Gentoo penguins
live on islands
near Antarctica.

King penguin chicks have brown feathers.

The emperor penguin isn't the only **species** that huddles together. King penguin chicks also huddle. They live on islands off the coast of Antarctica. They huddle while their parents hunt for food. This keeps them warm. It may be months before their parents return.

PROTECTING CHICKS

Large birds hunt king penguin chicks. Huddling protects chicks from **predators**. Chicks are better protected when they are in a group.

Penguins are birds. Like all birds, they can get cold when they lose body heat. Antarctic penguins must survive harsh winters. They can't lose too much body heat. It is a matter of life and death.

COOLING OFF

Some penguins live in warm places such as Australia. These penguins can get too hot. They hold their flippers out at their sides. Sea breezes cool them.

Penguins that live in cold places, such as emperor penguins, keep together to stay warm.

13

CHAPTER 3

FEATHER
Coats

Penguins have many ways of keeping warm. Feathers help them stay warm. Penguins have short feathers. They have a layer of soft, fluffy feathers next to their skin. This is called down. Down feathers stop heat loss. They protect penguins from cold.

Penguins puff their feathers out. This traps warm air between their feathers and skin. It keeps in body heat. Water can't enter this air space.

The down of a rockhopper penguin chick helps keep it warm.

Two king penguins oil their feathers.

A penguin has a **gland** near its tail. The gland makes oil. The penguin dips its beak in the oil. It spreads the oil over its feathers. The oil makes the top layer of feathers **waterproof**. Then water can't soak into the penguin's feathers. This helps the penguin glide through the water. It also keeps the penguin warm.

A gentoo penguin
basks in the sunlight.

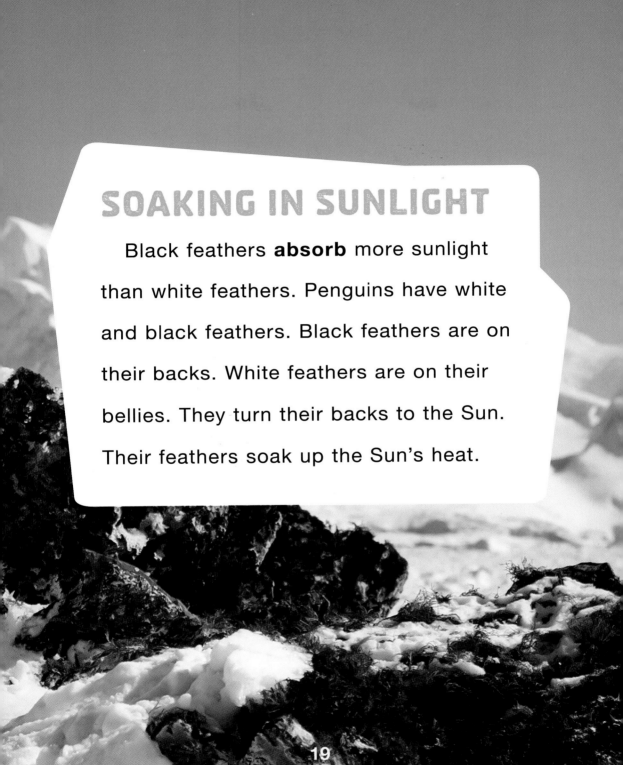

SOAKING IN SUNLIGHT

Black feathers **absorb** more sunlight than white feathers. Penguins have white and black feathers. Black feathers are on their backs. White feathers are on their bellies. They turn their backs to the Sun. Their feathers soak up the Sun's heat.

MOULTING

Penguin feathers become worn and damaged over time. Penguins **moult** once a year. This lets them replace old feathers. New feathers grow under the old ones. The new ones push the old ones out. Penguins lose feathers in patches.

A king penguin's
feathers look
different after
its first moult.

All penguins, including the rockhopper penguin, swim in cool waters. Blubber and waterproof feathers keep penguins warm.

Penguins need to keep warm while moulting. They eat a lot of food before they moult. They hunt for fish and other animals. This helps them build up fat.

This layer of fat is called **blubber**. Blubber acts like a blanket. It keeps penguins warm.

Feathers help penguins stay warm in cold water. But penguins lose feathers when they moult. So they stay on land and do not hunt for food. It takes up to three weeks to grow new feathers. During this time, they dont eat. Then they return to the water.

CHAPTER 4

KEEPING EGGS
Warm

Female penguins lay eggs. Emperor and king penguins lay one egg. They cover their eggs with their pouches. King penguins take turns doing this. Both males and females keep the eggs warm. Emperor penguins do not take turns. Male emperor penguins keep the eggs warm. Females leave to find food.

A chick later hatches from the egg.

It huddles in a parent's pouch. This helps

keep it warm.

King penguins
guard their
eggs carefully.

25

Gentoo penguins make their nests out of stones.

Other penguin species lay two eggs. They make nests. They gather rocks into piles. They put the eggs in the middle. They sit on the eggs. Males and females take turns. This keeps the eggs warm.

Penguins live in many places. Some live in Antarctica. Others live in warmer places. But all penguins swim in cool waters. All penguins need ways to stay warm. Their survival depends on it.

PENGUIN SPECIES

There are 18 species of penguins. Emperor penguins are the largest. Adults may weigh more than 36 kilograms (80 pounds).

GLOSSARY

absorb
to soak or take in

blubber
a layer of fat underneath
the skin

chick
a young penguin

down
soft and fluffy feathers

gland
an organ that produces a
certain substance in the body

moult
to shed feathers and grow
new ones

pouch
a pocket of featherless
skin that keeps penguin
chicks and eggs warm

predator
an animal that kills and eats
other animals

species
a group of animals that are
similar to each other

waterproof
not letting water through

TOP FIVE REASONS WHY
PENGUINS
ARE AWESOME

1. Penguins release air bubbles from their feathers when they swim. This helps them swim quickly.

2. Emperor penguins can dive more than 460 metres (1,500 feet) deep. They can stay underwater for nearly 30 minutes.

3. A penguin has a gland that filters salt from its blood. This allows it to drink salt water.

4. Penguins can adjust blood flow to their feet. This keeps their feet a few degrees above freezing. That way, their feet don't get stuck to the ice.

5. Some penguins swim at speeds of 35 kilometres (22 miles) per hour.

ACTIVITY

Blubber keeps penguins warm. You can try an experiment to learn how this works:

WHAT YOU WILL NEED

1 bowl

cold water (enough to fill the bowl)

3–4 ice cubes

a stopwatch

butter

paper towels

vegetable oil

lotion

INSTRUCTIONS

1. Work with a partner. Fill the bowl with cold water and the ice cubes.

2. Put your hand in the bowl. Ask your partner to use the stopwatch to time you for five seconds. Then remove your hand from the water and dry it.

3. Coat your hand with a layer of butter. Try another five seconds while your partner times you. Then remove your hand. Wash off the butter and dry your hand with paper towels.

Was your hand warmer with or without the butter? Try coating your hand with other substances, such as vegetable oil or lotion. Which substance do you think will keep you the warmest? Why do you think this is?

31

FIND OUT MORE

Penguins live all over the world! Check out these resources to learn about different penguin species.

Books

Penguins (Usborne Beginners), Emily Bone (Usborne, 2009)

Penguins, Anne Schreiber (National Geographic Kids, 2009)

Websites

DK Find Out! Emperor Penguin
www.dkfindout.com/us/animals-and-nature/birds/emperor-penguin/

National Geographic: Adélie Penguin
kids.nationalgeographic.com/animals/adelie-penguin/#adelie-penguin-jumping-
ocean.jpg

National Geographic: Penguins Do the Wave to Keep Warm
video.nationalgeographic.com/video/news/antarctica-emperor-penguins-
huddle-vin

INDEX